Notes from
a camper van

Alwyn Marriage

Bellhouse Books

First published in 2014 by Bellhouse Books, Guildford
www.bellhousebooks.wordpress.com

Copyright © 2014 Alwyn Marriage
ISBN 978-0-9930443-0-4

Printed in Great Britain by imprint digital, Devon

for Hugh

Acknowledgements

On the way to somewhere else was chosen to be
one of the Poems on the Buses in Guernsey, 2014,
and was read by the poet at the 2014 Guernsey
Literature Festival.
Road haul was commended in the Hastings
International Poetry Competition, 2012, and
published in Broadsheet 2014.
Spring camping and *Riding the storm* were both
published by the on-line poetry magazine, Nutshells
and Nuggets, in 2014.

Contents

En route

Everyone tries to overtake us
on the motorway,
obviously assuming that
a small converted camper van
will struggle up the hills;

they're clearly unaware
that our two point five litre
turbo-diesel engine
is built for business –
and much pleasure.

On the way to somewhere else

on the far side of the field
cars and lorries thunder past
in both directions

if each destination is equally
desirable, why didn't we all stay
just where we were before?

the field is bathed in cowslips,
bordered in a frill of blackthorn white
and ripe with birdsong under a blue sky

each spot we spend the night is where
we want to be, and in another sense
is simply on the way to somewhere else.

Spring camping

We headed west to Wales
this year to celebrate
a special birthday, stunned
by the sheer intensity of April
blazing in wild daffodil, in celandine
and buttercup; in countless sharp stars
piercing midnight's infinity;
and in the bone-numbing cold
of pre-dawn darkness.

Sherpa

Our last camper van
was full of charm and looked
as though it had escaped
from Toy Town.

The inside of this tardis was larger than the outside,
held enough clothes to last for many weeks,
all neatly stowed in roomy cupboards;
and over the front seats it even sported
a sunshine roof which we could open,
close or cover with a blind.
Best of all, it was the only van I've ever found
that had a fitted bookcase.

We bought it second-hand, but nearly new,
and even then its pace was elderly, sedate.
We didn't want to dash around the country
at high speed, but this was ultra-slow
by anybody's reckoning.

I finally flipped when driving home one day
I was overtaken by a milk float, going up a hill;
so in desperation we booked into a garage
to have the sluggish engine turbo charged,
then with gritted teeth we gripped
our seat belts as the van took off
at higher speed, clearly in search
of adventure.

Several years of camping later
the nights were fine, relaxed
and adequately spacious;
but it didn't seem entirely right that where
the rust had eaten at the metal floor,
we could watch the road pass by beneath our feet.

An amicable separation

Dear friend, It seems the time has come
for a parting of our ways. No malice,
not even disappointment, just
a mutual moving on.

We always knew there'd be an end
to our long, sweet relationship;
a time to say goodbye before we lost
the charm of all the memories we share.

We've spent so many nights together, wrapped
in peaceful sleep or watching through long hours
the passionate infinity of silent stars
that multiplied before our stretching eyes.

I've whispered my poetry and philosophy
into your midnight stillness, darkness
deepening our embrace as we both dreamt
of nothing except how good it was to be alive.

But moth and rust now threaten to erode
our trust, as they destroy your bodywork
and your faithful diesel engine finally protests
and splutters into rest.

*We finally parted company with our old Sherpa camper van when we
found we could watch the road going past under our feet through the rust
holes.*

Packed

for camping in our tiny van we pack
only the bare essentials, but are still surprised
to find the list so long:

Our ten-tog duvet,
towels and tea towel,
toothbrush, toothpaste, soap;

as many pairs of pants as days
we expect to camp, plus one
just in case we stay away

longer than expected;
jeans and jumpers, shorts and fleeces
to cover us and all eventualities;

walking boots and socks
and OS maps of all the places
we think we might be visiting;

wedge-shaped chocks for levelling the van
on sloping ground, a waterproof-backed rug
for poking underneath, between the wheels,

or lying in the sun (while someone else
is poking underneath the van);
a spanner and a screwdriver,

the jack and, for the continent,
emergency triangle and dayglow jacket;
our bird book and a guide to wayside flowers,

an illustrated volume on wild eating
and as an extra precaution when we're foraging,
a full-colour exhaustive field guide to wild fungi;

a penny whistle, as there's no room for my guitar,
a compact library uploaded to my tablet
with a plentiful supply of ibooks;

fresh water, instant coffee, long-life milk,
cereal, a tin of ratatouille and (of course)
a bottle of good wine.

GPS

That other woman in your car
always makes it clear that she knows best:
Continue 5.7 miles on the motorway she orders,
and because there isn't any other option,
you do as she says.

She's bossy and insensitive, lacks sympathy
for your mistakes, shows no respect
for you or for your passengers,
pours scorn on my map-reading
and has never introduced
an interesting topic of conversation
or shown any interest in your life.

In point eight of a mile, keep right
she chimes and, despite your life-long
left-leaning tendencies, you obediently
nose out towards the A road's central lane.

She's clearly got you hooked. Does she enjoy
the power she holds over you? *Continue
20 miles on M5 (or 6 or 20)*; *Perform
a legal U-turn*; or if she's feeling slightly
more polite: *Please drive to highlighted route.*

Amazed, I watch you meekly follow
her directions with no sign of argument
or irritation. I can't believe
the fundamental change I see in you,
and marvel at this new relationship.
You clearly trust a distant satellite
more than you trust your wife.

Free camping

But if you don't normally go to campsites,
where do you spend the night?

Deep in a wood, where there's just a chance
fairies or other elfin folk might arrive to dance
at midnight; along a public but unfrequented drive
edged with Queen Anne's Lace, where we believe
no one will disturb us; by a beach, beside
a deserted lake; high up on a mountain side
reached by interminable hair-pin bends
with corners that hover where the safe land ends.
Sometimes an empty lay-by on a quiet lane
or a deserted car park is enough for us to gain
a peaceful night; and once we parked in an empty space
outside a French cathedral, where we slept in peace.
In our best camping spots, fresh air and freedom sing,
no one knows where we are, and we don't need anything.

Road haul

we'd passed two
pheasants and a mangled
badger on the road
already: food
for buzzards and
for carrion crows

as we slowed the car
and turned into a narrow lane
we saw a third cock pheasant
lifeless in our track

there wasn't any doubt
that it was dead
the red and green and purple
sun-polished to a vibrant shine
above a field of corn
were dull, no movement
of a wing or feather's
flicker

so what strong instinct
made me steer the van
around the bird,
brushing the hedgerow as
I edged it past,

unnecessarily pleading innocence,
proving to anyone who might be interested
that there was no blood
on my wheels?

Bird hide

We park at low tide, just above the line
of seaweed stranded high and dry,
open the salt-sprayed window in the hope
that wading birds will be revealed;
but the mud that stretches out before us
is empty, desolate.

In the absence of avian interest we train
our binoculars onto acres of marine
grasses and interminable reeds.
Beyond the mudflats lawned with nitrates,
the single sail of a shallow-draughted boat
can just be seen.

Once, we watched red phalarope
swimming within three metres of our van,
and several times we've caught sight of an osprey;
but today there's nothing doing, so we close the window,
to warm ourselves and dispel disappointment
with a cup of tea.

Elevating

Look at this snail, and very gently touch
the topmost tip of its long tentacles.
See how instantly the horns retract, withdrawing
tender eyes into snug safety in its shell.

Similarly, when the wind is blowing
too hard for our comfort,
we simply drop the elevating roof
and slide into our bed.

A dream of blue

In May a sea of blossoms in the woods
bathed our eyes in blue, while in the garden
spikes reached up towards a matching sky
and intricate bells swelled and frilled around
their delicate pale stamens.

Arriving on high moorland in a June night's
fading light, the detail of the flora on the ground
around was bleached of colour, scents
swept away by wind. We slept.

Woken by skylarks, we looked out
to find our van embraced by tiny bluebells
pushing through coarse grass and bracken stalks,
nodding their agreement to the day.

Riding the storm

We've spent nights squeezed
in tiny cabins, tossing
on rough seas.

So as the rain descends, and water levels
rise, I wonder when the waves
will start to rock us.

breakfast al fresco

Yesterday the tarmac melted
on the road, the queue of traffic
stretched for twenty miles,
and dirty exhaust
streamed from the ears
of angry motorists

then this morning
we sat outside the van
on moorland, eating
breakfast in the huge
silence punctuated only
by rippling skylark song.

No overnight camping

No watching for badgers or listening for owls tonight; no
lying starstruck gazing at infinity, with darkness wrapping
round the windows, preventing our cosy warmth and
awestruck astronomy from leaking out.

This impenetrable height-bar set at six foot six is far too low
for us to pass; we couldn't duck under, skirt around or
squeeze beneath Eden's flaming sword, even if we released
the air from all our tyres and held our breath.

A height bar should be high, close to the sky, not so low,
down-in-the-dumps and scrape the ground, decapitate
unwary vans.

Firmly excluded from this beauty spot are gypsies and
travellers, families in caravans, white van men and other
undesirables, including two law-abiding citizens in a tiny
camper, who had hoped to enjoy a peaceful night under the
shining stars.

Yet despite the unwelcoming sign, it should be obvious
to anyone who thinks, that our presence in the car park
overnight would be a deterrent to criminals who love
to gravitate to such deserted places for their nefarious deeds.

Camping with a cafetière

After years of tipping half-drunk mugs
of instant coffee down the drain,
we finally rewarded our camper van
with its very own cafetière.

Camping breakfasts were immediately
transformed as fine aromas
of Kenyan, Columbian or Costa blend
wafted over the morning air

waking our taste buds, while gently
opening our eyes to the day,
comforting us with familiar tastes
that can now be enjoyed anywhere.

Party night

Instead of parking at the village hall
we stopped beside the entrance to a cornfield,
and walked the last half mile.

We ate and drank and danced till late,
raised our voices over mounting decibels
of revellers in competition with canned music;

then as the moon rose high we said
farewell and slipped away to enjoy the peace
of a star-lit walk towards our waiting bed.

Transported

Hanging from the camper van's rear window
our bicycles are transported to wild and remote places,
where every moorland track and quiet lane will lead us
to beach or waterfall or perfect picnic spot.

One bright and breezy Hebridean day
we left our two bikes where the lane gave out
to dunes, and climbed to find a high position
with a clearer view over the beach below.

We sat and watched wild otters play
on clean white sand, then tumble into waves
to fish for unsuspecting prey, quite unaware
of eyes that watched them swimming,

then slinking up the rocks
to eat their catch,
small red tongues clearly visible
as they sat and picnicked in the sun.

On the way back to where the van was parked
we met two broad and blue-eyed men
unpacking from their fishing boat
their day's harvest of crab.

After chatting, they insisted we accept
a generous gift, then cheered us on
as we rode away, each with two wriggling
plastic bags hanging from our handlebars.

Good morning, Mt Blanc

We wake to find the sun is creeping
stealthily down the slope. Deep shadows
hug the edges of rough outcrops, and the sky
is hard, bright, full-of-promise blue.

Our balloons of used-up breath
have gathered overnight, and failing to escape
have formed a series of cooperative rivulets
leaking down the inside of the windows.

Night of noisy waterborne peace
emerges into glorious morning.
Dressing underneath the now warm duvet
we plan the day's adventures,

while emerging from the rock-face opposite,
a silver thread expands into a veil
before falling several thousand feet to join
the already full and thrashing stream below.

Slowly, surreptitiously, the sun slithers towards us,
swallowing shadows as it hungrily
licks the rough grey granite
and the few brave trees.

Stray wisps of cloud float overhead,
one looks for all the world
just like a giant thumbprint
smudged onto the sky.

Inside the cramped one-body space,
we move around each other in a dance;
while to our east the peak occludes
the sun, which undeterred

creeps down the westward mountain
inch by inch
in an unhurried march to reach
and warm our van.

High solitude

Four and a half thousand feet up on the flanks
of Mt Blanc, we battened down the roof
and snuggled underneath our ten tog duvet.
I pulled a fleecy cap down round my head, and slept.

The moon was full, flooding us with white
and covering the granite cliff with dreams of snow.
The raging torrent beside us never paused in gathering
fresh supplies of water to hurl down towards the sea.

A sudden shriek: was it a bird or mammal?
Snug in the safety of our bed we listened
to unidentified scurrying underneath the floor
and pattering of avian feet across the roof.

Night noises

A soft whistle interrupting
the midnight peace is followed by
indignant sleep-drugged chirps,
before another bird emits
a low monotonous
but strangely meditative
chk, *chk*, chewing on
a problem all night long.

We hear an owl's cry
mocking through the woods,
but fail to catch the answering
shriek of terror, or see
the frantic patter of tiny feet
losing this last race.

Stripey

The road ahead is striped,
red on the left in front and white
approaching on the right.

Receding, a twinkling caterpillar
sidles sideways past the stream
of harsh bright beams.

We follow in its wake, averting eyes
to dodge the constant dazzle
as dragons charge towards us.

Reading the signs

Travelling westwards on the M4 motorway
a sign instructs us to *Turn R for the Oracle.*
Will there, I wonder, be queues to consult
this Delphic sage? and can I ask
what my future holds?

Along the lane there's evidence of recent
road works, and another sign that reads
Cats' Eyes Removed. I wonder what
a foreigner's supposed to make of that;
is it a threat or promise?

Messages on the move

Nearly every vehicle that takes its place
on the motorway in front of us
delivers a different message through
communication on the rear view window:

Don't follow me, I'm lost, Green army,
Support our lifeboats, Caring for cats.
We keep our windows unfashionably clear,
communicating with each other

through the medium of voice and ear,
and no one following has any idea
what either of us is thinking,
or even who we are.

Harvest time
Our friends the farmers

It's a sunny Saturday in summer, so of course
the local farmer needs to bring his tractor out
to pull the most enormous load of hay
six miles along this busy road
to where a neighbouring farmer lives,

who would have welcomed his hay-bearing friend,
except that he's also coupled up and making
his own slow and steady way along
the single carriage section of the road,
pulling a container of twenty sheep to meet
their future owners or succumb to slaughter.

Revving impatiently at a junction
we catch sight of a dilapidated tractor
pulling a steaming cart of stinking muck
that leaves a slimy trail of effluent
for miles along the road behind.
This, strangely, serves to reassure us
that our piled-up hay bales
may not be quite so bad.

We wonder who has managed to collect
the richest and most satisfying harvest.
Maybe the other farmer with his attendant sheep
has attracted a longer line of traffic; but in our queue
there's an over-heating souped-up Mercedes,
two land rovers pulling caravans,
several more motor campers and a stream
of cars of assorted size and colour,
whose drivers are coping to greater or lesser
degree with the irritation of being stuck
in the heat of the day
behind a slowly moving load of hay.

But at least there are two happy farmers
out enjoying the summer weather
and their sunny Saturday harvest.

Red eyes at night

We drove for hours on the motorway
following paired red lights
on fast retreating cars,
that peered back at us through
the darkness as they fled.

Later, down a winding lane,
darkness thickening like blood,
two bright red eyes
stared out from the undergrowth
that cloaks the verge.

Romantic about Romanies

My mother said, that I never should ...
and yet they held me spellbound;
I wanted to go with them
wherever that might be,
to unknown and exotic ground
over the hills and far away.

I longed for a swarthy stranger
with dark brown twinkling eyes
to carry me off through charm or force
from the safe, tame confines of my home,
in a gaily painted caravan
drawn by a fetlocked horse.

My sister's disused doll's pram,
two buckled bicycle wheels,
and even the baby's old tin bath,
circled wildly in my childish mind
before re-forming and transforming
into the chariot of my dreams.

And now we spend whole summers
out under the stars, forget
the comfort of mattress, shower and larder,
embrace the joys of romantic freedom
before abandoning our gypsy life
with an autumnal tinge of regret.

Technological limits

With my accelerator foot I send
a squirt of diesel oil into the cylinders
just beyond the dashboard,
where pistons put it under pressure,
squeezing until the fuel explodes
into a release of power,
proving that the movement of my foot
is closely connected to our forward motion.

Intake, compression, power, exhaust:
the words, the sequence and the process
all make clear mechanical sense;
and if one day the van broke down,
maybe even I could don some rubber gloves,
peer underneath the bonnet, fiddle around
with nuts and bolts until I found the cause
then, referring to the instruction manual
for a four stroke engine, rectify the problem.

In the passenger seat, I rest
an iPad on my lap,
connected to worlds I do not know
and cannot understand,
where particles are dashing round
at unimaginable speeds
without the sort of clash that in a car
would certainly cause
a crash.

With my finger I demand
directions to the place I want
to go and trace the road I wish
to take. Then for light relief
I glance at photos of my family
and listen through an earplug
to the podcast of a programme
aired on the radio a year ago.

But if the screen grew blank
and failed to operate,
while the sound of the programme
I was listening to began to die away,
there's nothing I could do to restore
this non-mechanical machine to functionality.
In my frustration I could shake it, bang it,
search its intimate interior with the aid
of screwdriver and magnifying glass,
but I doubt if it would ever release its secrets
or deign to give me the satisfaction
of hearing it creak and groan back into life.

Not my choice of camping spot

No, I'm not prepared to camp tonight
underneath a pylon.
It may be late, I realise
we've been searching in the dark
for a suitable spot to stop
for three quarters of an hour.
But why should we endure
the constant hum of electrical activity
below the conscious level,
or have our brains deep-fried
while sleeping. I don't care
if there isn't any scientific evidence:
I just know that what descends on me
from these megaliths of power
is generally increased tension
and a headache.

Woof woof grrr

Having found this deserted corner of the moors
in the quietness of fading light last night,
we were surprised to be woken by an army
of dog-walkers, parking their cars around our van
and striding out in all directions, hurling balls
from flexible plastic catapults. Our peace
was shattered by wild yaps of happiness,
immediately followed by fierce growls and barks
as these docile companions met with other members
of the canine species.

Whose turn to drive?

If I take over driving for a while
you can sleep, or shave or have a snack.
You've driven a hundred miles today already
and I know it isn't fair to leave it all to you;

but if you drive
I can sit beside you
writing more poetry.

Beach hut

Autumn has started, all the best
sandy beaches are deserted,
and though the sun still shines,
the wind blows chill.

Keen to maintain our daily swim
we put the roof up, change
then leave our clothes behind, and dash
down across the beach into the waves

where we cavort and spin, our strokes
now faster, as is our exit when
we rush back to the welcome warmth
of our private changing room beside the sea.

Campsite

The season's over, we're
the only people on the campsite,
choose a spot perched high above
the lake in an enfolding circle
of blue hills, where convent bells
echo over water, and emerging
lights reflected from the far
shore shimmer like electric
glow worms, mirroring
each slow and silent star.

Withdrawal symptoms

We've given up the gypsy life
as winter swallows what was left
of long warm light-filled evenings,
and mornings when the early sunshine
found a welcoming crack between our curtains
where they don't quite meet.

It may be cold, but rather than
free camping in the snow
maybe we could book into a campsite
– if there's one still open –
connect to an electric hook-up
to power our old fan heater,
go out to dinner in a local pub
then tuck ourselves up very early
underneath thirteen togs.

G Hugh at 70

and Jehu drove furiously (2 Kings 9: 20)

It's slower than a tortoise
but faster than a hare,
and no one expects drivers to lower
their speed to just *ten* miles an hour
when driving on an open road;
though when squeezing through
a narrow gate or reversing
it's not such a bad idea.

Home zones hum with human activity
and the patter of tiny creatures
who haven't learnt their highway code
and therefore need some means of traffic calming
to protect them from thoughtless vehicles
that might be tempted to travel faster
than *twenty* miles an hour.

Thirty is a safe and sensible
limit worth observing
in English towns and villages
and narrow country lanes.
Sometimes bumps and zigzags
as we enter a restricted zone
remind us that busy shoppers
as well as children and the old
have a right to safety
and every house is someone's home.

On roads that join these centres
of slow and steady civilization,
we accelerate to *forty*,
sniff a whiff of future speed,
aim for dual carriageways,

check the hand brake is released
and fail to watch the trembling arrow
as it rises surreptitiously
towards a penalty point.

Fifty drags us to a standstill
on motorways where roadworks,
accidents or adverse weather
conditions slow the traffic.
What once seemed fast and free
now drags and irritates,
but if we keep our heads,
and hold our horses,
we'll probably arrive no later
that expected.

It's worth remembering
on the open road
that unless you're on a motorway
the speed limit is *sixty*.
Our engine begs to be allowed
to accelerate away, but conscience,
not to mention the occasional camera,
suggests it might be wise to follow
the instructions in the highway code.

As miles and years fly by and lie
behind us it's been possible to test
what speeds and modes of transport suit us best,
enabling us to reach our destination safely.
Personally, I prefer a pace
that allows me to enjoy the scenery
as we drive; but rest assured,
I will still love you at *seventy*.

on into the future

Planning holidays
with a taste for adventure
we'll camp together

fresh air and deep sleep
passion and conversation
blessing our journeys.